Voice Mail

Duncan Forbes

Voice Mail

ENITHARMON PRESS

2002

First published in 2002
by the Enitharmon Press
26B Caversham Road
London NW5 2DU

www.enitharmon.co.uk

Distributed in the USA and Canada
By Dufour Editions Inc.
PO Box 7, Chester Springs
PA 19425, USA

Text © Duncan Forbes 2002
Cover image © David Hockney 2002

ISBN 1 900564 92 0

British Library Cataloguing-in-Publication Data.
A catalogue record for this book is available
from the British Library.

Typeset in Bembo by Servis Filmsetting Ltd
and printed in England by
The Cromwell Press

Contents

La Brea 9
Anno Domini 11
Brinkburn Priory 13
Hothouse at Wallington 14
Severn Bore 15
New Year's Eve 16
Misery 16
Job Description 17
Melissani 18
Ithaka 20
Animal Passion 21
It 22
Ipomea 24
Alec 25
Father 26
Happiness 30
Good Friday 31
Enigma 32
Sub-Minoan 34
Reprisals 35
Mission 37
Güzelyurt 38
Eclipse 39
Dragonfly 40
Holly 41
Day at the Dewhursts 42
Combing the Beach 46
Breaking the Silence 47
Bougainvillaea 48
Bombylans 49
Beached 50
Looking for Driros 51
Auspice 53

Arrivals 54
Arykanda 56
Anubis and the Wet Nurse 58
Memento 59
Auntie Millie 61
Niagara 63
Ghost Town 64
Open 365 Days 65
At Pismo Beach 66
Pacific 67
Petrified Forest 69
San Francisco Bay 70
Agave Americana 71
America 72
A Better Berry 73
Spring 74
Seed 75
A Burnt Out Case 76
Appointment 77
The Shade of Sir John Betjeman Revisits Bletchley, Bucks. 78
No Time Wasters Please 79
Sometimes 81
Song of Innocence and Inexperience 82
Impasse 83
Insomnia 84
Nature of the Art 85
Inconsequence 86
Origin of the Species 87
Shark 88

Snakes and Meteors 89
Two Tigers 91
Vision Mixer 94
Zoological Gardens 95
Sunday at Messanges
 Plage 97
The Great Pirarucu 98
Thesaurus 99
Thought 100
Hong Kong Island 101
A Million Licensed
 Guns 102
United Nations 104
Wild West 106
After the Sermon 108
Best Before End 109
Bloodsucker 109
Chapter One 110
Equal Opportunism 111
Common or Garden 112
Neighbourhood Watch 113
Not Today 114
Target 116

Tears 117
Downing Street Cat 119
Euroland 121
Seeing the Light 123
Sitting on the Harbour
 Wall 124
On Both Fronts 125
Next of Kin 127
Presences 128
Rio Ter 129
Watercolour 130
Parc Liais 131
Welcome 132
Exit 133
Why Can't I Be Poet
 Laureate? 135
Wine and Cheese 136
Self-Deceit 137
Cyclical 138
Song 140
Fair Copy 141
'A poem written in
 blood' 143

Let us imagine that the sight of the things that surround us is not familiar, that it is only allowed us as an exception, and that we only obtain it by a miracle, knowledge of the day, of human beings, of the heavens, of the sun, and of faces. What would we say about these revelations, and in what terms would we speak of this infinity of wonderfully adjusted data? What would we say of this distinct, complete and solid world, if this world only appeared very occasionally, to cross, to dazzle, and to crush the unstable, incoherent world of the solitary soul?

PAUL VALÉRY

La Brea

I am the tarred and feathered stork
Who flapped its limbs until they stuck.

I am a tapir ancestor
Who came for water, swallowed tar.

This is the asphalt killing-ground,
A lake that thirsts. Beware. Be warned.

His trunk a blowhole out of reach,
A mammoth trumpets liquid pitch.

We are a pack of dire wolves
Who scented death and mired ourselves.

I am the grief of a giant sloth
Who drank the waters of black death.

Lion and lioness salivate
At bison ready trapped to eat.

Coyote, jaguar and puma
Die for a taste of dying llama.

A squirrel bleating in distress
Allures a rattlesnake to death.

The tar immobilizes both
The short-faced bear and sabretooth.

The water winnows skeletons
Caught in a trap of sun and rain.

I am the skull of the only human,
Anonymous La Brea Woman.

The sump of ancient swamp-remains
Swallows the battles of old bones.

The eagle and the condor drown
In liquid nightfall underground.

Anno Domini

Beyond both Alnmouth and the Aln,
Above a boat-filled estuary,
A cross stands on a mound or dune
Like a cathedral drowned in sand,
A small hill for a Calvary
Up which a figure in the sun
Climbs to the top, then kneels in prayer,
As if she were illusory,
A pilgrim from an earlier age
Or apparition on a screen,
Dressed in the habit of a nun.

But kneeling there she joins her hands,
Bows to the cross to meditate,
Then wanders to the water's edge,
Takes off her shoes and cools her feet
Where North Sea meets Northumberland.

And we that evening walk around
The saltmarsh, as the sun goes down,
To find the ruins of a shrine
With Saxon carvings on the arch.
We take a sandpath up the mound
To touch the upright of the cross
And read the letters round the base:
St Cuthbert A.D. and a date,
A founding father of the church
Whose landfall it commemorates
In silent stone above a beach.

Above the beach in silent stone,
The halo of a harvest moon
Illuminates the planet's rim
And worshipping the setting sun
The tidal waters seem to flame.

Brinkburn Priory

A doorway through a Norman arch.
Whispers echo at the silence,
Eyes adjusting to the dark
In cellar smells of ancient stonework
Void of worshippers and pews.
Sunlight through the stained-glass windows
Glazes terracotta tiles.
A bird is flying in the rafters.
Wildflowers drying on the altar
Are ragwort, knapweed, willowherb.

The Risen Christ by Fenwick Lawson,
Born in 1932,
Dominates the northern transept:
Displaying hands in benediction,
A giant airborne monk in beechwood
Hangs aloof on chains and metal.
Strange to find the resurrection
Signified by weight of wood:
Apotheosis of a tree-trunk
Posing as a rib of God.

Two girls are playing in the garden
With a remnant of fraying rope,
Moles have undermined the lawn,
Rosebay willowherb in sunlight
Seeds along the riverbank;
The water, noisy as a torrent,
Carves its channel out of sight.
Beech trees dominate the valley
Witnessing a prehistoric
Resurrection into leaf.

Hothouse at Wallington

Willowherb in the guttering
Is bowing to the wind and rain
Outside the warm conservatory
In which a giant fuchsia tree
Has lived a century or more
And, buzzing to its crimson bell,
A bee is entering a flower
Which looks like a gloxinia.

Northumberland as South of France?
The plundering of India?
Photographers seem unaware
What engineering works have done
With money, metal, wood and glass
To simulate or reproduce
Warm climates in this latitude's
Utopia or paradise.

So do not ask or look askance
At the desire to interfere
With people, culture, creatures, weather:
Enjoy the cornucopia's
Rich aristocracy of plants
And hope the worker bee escapes
Through air-vents to the open air
Of willowherb and moorland heather.

Severn Bore

Flowing muddily through the meadows
Past orchards, cows and banks of clay,
Past shivering trees' inverted shadows,
The Severn broadens on its way.

Funnelled as if towards a sluice,
Bara, a billow from Old Norse,
Spreads rapidly across the Noose
Its equinoctial tidal force.

A noisy train at Minsterworth,
It rounds the corner with a swerve,
A wall of water and a wave
Drenching the willows with brown surf.

Shipping the driftwood back upstream
With smells of estuary and reeds,
It fills the channel like a reen
And still the water levels rise

As if it ran away from sea
And half the ocean were to come
Collapsing on the valley trees
In a catastrophe of foam.

And there look up! The daylight moon
Oblivious to all these words
Floats like the North Atlantic's brain
And floods a river in reverse.

New Year's Eve

On this, the last day of the year,
That now inseparable pair
Like crescent moon and evening star,
Both metal-bright and crystal-clear
Against a blue crepuscular,
Enact their dance of near and far
Prehistories of the calendar
Before they seem to disappear,
A sickle and a nymphaea
Into the cold December air.

Misery

I've caught the train to Misery.
I know each stop and station:
Regret, Remorse and Jealousy,
Revenge and Resignation.

There's no escape across the sea:
An airline takes you there.
The pilot is despondency,
The passenger despair.

Job Description

Dogsbody. Despot. Saint and martyr.
Diplomat. Bureaucrat. Creep and tartar.
Tamer of lions, cobra-charmer.
Nuclear warhead and disarmer.
Expert with parents, sons and daughters,
Weasel words and troubled waters.
Menagerie manager/manageress,
A human dynamo hooked on stress.
An innovative facilitator,
Proactive professional loyalist traitor.
Workaholic with sense of balance,
Renaissance figure with multi-talents,
Gravitas and a winning smile,
Impeccable manners and perfect style.
A drudge, a drone, a worker ant,
A meek impoverished sycophant
Who craves acceptance and admittance,
Suffers fools gladly, works for a pittance.
Name two referees, one of them God.
No weirdos please. Apply in blood.

Melissani

With a natural skylight of sky,
in a cave flamboyant with light,
the dancing of sun on water
projects a mural of flames
while a dry confetti of leaves
falls to the surface and floats
on astonishing green and blue
sapphire, viridian water,
the lapis and aquamarine
of microscope and planet
through which the limestones gleam
in water searching for sea
at a hundred litres per minute.

The standing taciturn Greek
with moustache and balding head
who leans on oars in the boat
is Charon rowing the ferry
and we are the shades in Hades,
a jostling crowd of tourists,
entering Stygian gloom
with flash photography,
noticing pigeons and bats
and mossy stalactites
as we travel the bottomless lake
to everlasting night.

Turn round before it's too late.
Re-enter the world of light,
the fig-tree on the island,
the ramp of waiting faces
and up the tunnel through rock
into the heat of sunlight
for a drink of cooling water
and cards to write to loved ones
from Melissani Lake.

ITHAKA

The cicadas are making arid rackets with their ratchets
in the olives and the pine trees
on the desiccated ground.
The randy sparrows scavenge ravenous for seeds
in the scrub of dried oregano, thyme and broom.
The swifts are dipping sipping water on the wing
in the insect-laden air.
The sea-urchins are clinging like burrs to the barnacled rocks.
And a ship at anchor is admiring in the mirror
its double on the water which is lapping at its sides dappled
with a mural of light-reflecting water.

And this is what we dream of when we dream of our return:
not the rocky, inhospitable
island of steep crags and brackish water
where weavers of wool and sheep-thieves
sleep impoverished in hovels
or like emaciated chickens
scratch a living from the earth,
but the familiar profile on the horizon
beyond the horizon
and all the people and the places
we have loved as if by birthright
ready to welcome a homecoming stranger.

Animal Passion

In the seaside villa of a nobleman
On holiday by the Ionian Sea,
The tesserae are savaging a youth
Who seems to acquiesce in the attack
Of rampant panther, leopard, tiger, lion,
Mosaic black in claw and white in tooth.
The artist Krateros has signed his work
And worded its significance in Greek.

It's strange to think that elegant young man
Should envy other people's happiness
And therefore is a human sacrifice
But he's the only pebble on the beach
And like the lunar pebble in the sky
He longs for water which he cannot reach.
In another panel in a nearby room
Two votarists prepare to stun and knife
A lapidary bull, a boar, a ram
And offer entrails to a stony flame.

It

An irritant like oyster grit,
It's highly wrought till Holy Writ.

It is a painting redesigned
By body language spirit mind.

It's like a drive through snow and sleet.
It's where you go and who you meet.

It's sacramental says the priest,
A sacrifice that serves a feast.

Both self-absorbed and self obsessed
It simulates an idle quest.

It's look-at-me while I exist,
Your modest exhibitionist.

Infinite talent for taking pains,
It profiteers and entertains.

By justifying every letter,
It leaves society the better.

As infantile as nursery play,
It is the ordure of the day.

Ephemeral and made to last,
It's icon and iconoclast,

A gift to the perfectionist
Where choice and chance can co-exist.

It's posthumous and future simple,
An afterlife of myth and symbol

Or else an offering, cult and votive,
The ultimate ulterior motive.

Ipomea

Pouting our love for the sky,
Quiet loudspeakers of blue,
We laud and magnify
Morning and morning dew.

My mother loved those flowers
And now I love them too,
Emblem of precious hours,
Sunlight and answering blue.

Alec

Throned in a wheelchair, mouth open, being fed
In paralytic second babyhood,
He smiles and winks but leaves the rest unsaid.
He knows he's talking scribble parrot-phrase
As words unravel in his addled head,
A tower of Babel in the Blitz ablaze.
Dementia has demeaned him and diminished
All memories of anyone he cherished.
(Who is that woman? Did I marry her?)
Deteriorating synapses have perished
All the co-ordinates of love and care.
Each day now is a sentence left unfinished.

Father

The skeleton in its shroud
and the skin on the head so cold,
the teeth in the mouth half open
as if to yawn or laugh,
and nose stuck in the air,
the death-mask stare of the eyes,
and typical wisps of hair
over the stone-cold scalp,
with a grandpaternal look
in a pose of imagined repose
under two paintings of yours,
The Roofs and *Coverack*
both from your palette-knife phase,
with two of your purchases:
the hunting esquimaux,
two huntsmen in canoes,
pursuing caribou
swimming white Arctic seas
and the land-hunt on the snow
in turquoise, pink and blue.

And so the memories stir
elsewhere in other time
of selves in another year
and I imagine you now,
a big man in your prime,
consultant and physician,
who would have ministered
to the old man in the bed
with quadriplegia,
dementia or whatever,
till he becomes once more
the handsome sporting hero

double-blue thwarted by war,
the Greyhound No 8
and freshman Magdalen oar.

The marriage to Norah Wilson,
the young Paulina girl
next door at Lexham Gardens
who tackled the arrogant chap
walking each day to St Paul's
in a tasselled rugby cap.

The Hausa Grammar, foxed
from his days as the 'plausible Major'
with the West Africa Corps
in Northern Nigeria till
bilharzia saved the doctor
from Burma and the war.

The conjurer who could
with a copper penny seem
to rub it behind his head,
then, with revolting mime
and hideous snorting noise,
forehead purple with strain,
sneeze through his hairy nose
the same unbloodied coin
with George VI who died
and Rule Britannia waves.

The wacky, eccentric don
who collected the works of Jung,
The Tibetan Book of the Dead,
Oudspensky and Gurdjieff,
a theosopher who read

Meister Eckhart and Freud,
Boehme and Swedenborg,
Lilliput and Dan Dare
in the *Eagle* before I did.

I could not now rehearse
those arguments we had,
philosophical battles,
typical son and dad
antler-locking rebuttals
of youth by adulthood
or was it the reverse:
the dogmatism of youth
and sceptical adult pride
locked in empirical proof?

The paterfamilias
at his most generous self
dispensing food and drink,
glass after excellent glass
of vintage Bordeaux wine
kept to its perfect time,
decanted with fuss and finesse
and warmed to an optimum.
Here's to our very good health
and bottle-filled cellar-shrine.

He who endowed me with life
looks like Brueghel's *Aveugle*
with his mouth half open to laugh
and his eyes' unseeing gaze.
The shape of the skull and the scalp
and the skull-cap cranium
round the brain which once contained
the names of every bone

in the body which lies so still
in rigor mortis repose.

I kiss the forehead farewell,
cold as a statue now,
the scalp and the cheeks are cool
and lifeless as the snow
or the huntsmen in canoes
pursuing caribou
across the Arctic seas
in turquoise, pink and blue.
So rare for the end to be
triumphant like the start,
So rare for the head to obey
the dictates of the heart.
Father, forgive, I pray.
Be near me now we part.

Happiness

If happiness writes white,
What is it, do you think?
Answers please, true or trite,
In permanent black ink.

I know what happiness is
And where it sometimes goes.
I have experienced bliss
And corresponding lows.

Its nutrients are hope,
Fidelity and love
And these in human shape
Bring happiness enough.

Good Friday

The smell of incense
perfumes open air,
the bearded priests
lift beaded crucifix
to cense and bless
the evening streets
and raise the cross
past balconies
where dames in black
who genuflect
and cross themselves
asperge the multitude
chanting in front
and chatting at the back.
Fat scented droplets
fall on cars and tarmac,
and harbour lights
are walking on the water
while we are following
like children at
a ceremonial
who understand
they understand
few fragments of the whole.

Enigma

In a basilica of air,
An ancient moon of sun-baked clay,
A terracotta text inscribed
Like flat earth and the turning globe,
Stares out at us with one blind eye.

Discovered in a mud-brick chest,
A cryptogram of hieroglyphs
In spirals on a two-faced disc
Thwarts scholar and philologist
With its elusive mysteries.

Revolve the symbols in the mind:
A goatskin rug and shield embossed,
Upstanding fish, farm implements,
A flower in blossom, grain and plants,
The crested head and walking man.

Retrace the spiral of the signs
From centre to circumference
And back again as in a dance.
Is it the lyric of a song,
A hymnal or a game of chance?

A walking man reads left to right
A series of dumb images
Surmising melodies for flute
Before the feathered myths took flight
And Christians realigned the fish.

Why do I look so long and hard
Almost with love and reverence
At these beginnings of the word,
While indecipherable stars
Assume their insignificance?

Sub-Minoan

The most beautiful
piece in the Archaeological
Museum is not
the bull's head
libation cup
in black steatite
nor the ivory acrobat,
the snake goddess,
octopus ceramics,
nor gold bee pendant,
though they are miracles
of creation, craftsmanship,
loss and retrieval,
but the young attendant
in Gallery XII,
poised on her chair
between pithoi
and sarcophagi.

Reprisals

The speeding car swerves to avoid
A Greek boy playing in the road.
He takes the child to look and see
Then breaks its arm across his knee.
This is the island where a bull
Inseminated Pasiphae.

That night the chauffeur we had coshed
Slid into semi-consciousness.
They shot him through the fractured skull
While kidnapped Major-general Kreipe
Became obsessive in his loss
Of general's cap and Iron Cross.

Along the labyrinthine paths,
We paid the brigands sovereign gold,
St George of England George VI,
And spoke to them in schoolboy Greek
Through Sophoclean idioms –
Such were our tender politics.

And would I do it all again?
The past recedes into a myth
Of anecdote and aftermath
Repeated by the photographs.

Paddy in German uniform
Playing the part with Aryan scorn.
The general on Mt Ida's slopes
Nursing with shame his dying hopes.
A Buchan tale of derring-do
Hailed as a propaganda coup.

But now the Nazi minotaur
Herr General Muller's back again
As tyrant and avenging god,
George is a prisoner-of-war
And natural justice for the Hun
Takes as reprisals ten for one.

I see a plain of smoking farms,
The villages reduced to flames,
The living flung in burning homes,
The dead contaminating streams,
The butchered sheep and frightened goats,
Betrayal and the firing squad.

Mission

Old woman crippled in a barrow,
A mother wailing out her sorrow,

And miles of destitute refugees
Patrolled by soldiers and police.

This is the birthright which we lost
When Ottomites invaded us.

Ruling with bullethole and semen,
They kill the men and rape our women.

If this can happen now to us,
There is no god and never was.

I Drita, not my real name,
Am bearing witness to their crime.

They asked which hand he practised with,
Then cut the doctor's fingers off.

President of the United States,
I dare not talk of hypocrites.

A family man in combat kit,
I pilot one of NATO's jets

Exploding into smithereeens
The target on a radar screen.

The darkened Danube, fast and cold,
Flows underneath our human shield.

Güzelyurt

Do you remember Güzelyurt?
'Quite nice and lovely,' said the guide,
though not a Turkish-Cypriot,
'and worth a journey to the west.'

And so we went on market day
to find, among the citrus fruit,
the lemons and the orange groves
that ran beside the scented road,

a market in a market town,
both ordinary and nondescript,
although it sold a vivid feast
of fishes, vegetables and fruit,

of butchered sheep and leather goods,
of nuts and raisins, leaves and roots,
and while we looked and wandered round
the men outside a café stared.

We wondered what we might have missed
beside the minaret and mosque
but I remember Güzelyurt,
though we were there an hour at most.

Eclipse

To celebrate their fire-on-stone
Anthropomorphic nuptial fling,
She wears an iridescent brooch
And non-existent diamond ring
With lunar valley necklace pearls
And golden bracelet round the bone
As tidal waters on the beach
Are agitated into foam.

While coronation of the moon
With crown of flames and ring of fire
Enacts a pageant of rebirth,
The sun becomes a crescent moon,
A furnace door of flaming mouth
Ingests a mandala of stone
And sun and moon are making love
Or so it seems from darkened earth.

As if it were a passing phase,
The sun emerges to ignite
The chemistry of genesis
On fields of gravity and light's
Historic choreographies
And then they go their separate ways,
The sun-god and the satellite,
Innumerable nights and days.

Dragonfly

With wings of tissue-paper quartz,
it dragonflies and dragonflits,

a bullet of metallic sheen,
a flying samurai machine,

a humming-bird on skimming flights,
then like a butterfly alights

and leans to drink from lily pads
libations offered to the gods,

a lace-winged ephemopteron
whose turquoise jewelled abdomen,

a photon of the worshipped sun,
shines iridescent and is gone.

Holly

November but the sky is blue.
Behind the holly stands a yew.
Beneath the leaves and clustered fruits
Grow unseen undertrees of roots.

I sit and watch a pigeon eat
Red holly berries raw as meat,
A plump grey cleric of a bird
If feral rock-dove sounds absurd.

It flaps and sidles, cranes its neck,
Eyeballs a berry, plucks and peck!
The leaves and shadows both vibrate
As bird unbalanced shifts its weight

Till branch and pigeon seem to come
Back to an equilibrium:
But why the pigeon or the tree?
Why fruit to beak or sky like sea?

The spread of seed and appetite,
The red on green or blue of light
Presume a visionary belief
As evergreen as any leaf.

Day at the Dewhursts

Little Lord Fauntleroy on a secondhand bike,
my first with gears, I cycled
through Crownhill with the parcel tied to crossbar,
the mileometer ticking surreptitiously.

I cycled through the village
of Tamerton Foliot,
with its four-square ancient stone
Devonian church
to the Dewhursts' dairy farm.

Charlie Fred, my friend and everyone's,
a handsome boy in a *Just William* way.
His younger sister, Sarah,
mother, and noisy farmer father, Colonel Fred,
gruff, hearty, bluff and military in moustache:
a living character from a Giles cartoon.

Their small farmhouse was lined improbably
with English Impressionist paintings, oils
of donkeys, orchards, woodland, all signed Dewhurst.

Together we explored the farm:
cowpats thick with dung flies
and duckweed in the ditches,
the Land-Rover with its two tanks of petrol,
the outhouses, the stables and the sheds,
tall leather riding boots on wooden legs,
the generator with its oily smell
and the dark secret of the gelding iron
which Charlie Fred showed me how to use,
or claimed to, with a piece of grass
and polythene.

We watched their randy ram
who had a reputation as a stud
so we admired his pendulous
black scrotum and gross testicles
and waited for him to father many lambs,
but he just chewed grass, tearing at the tufts,
and seemed as bored by grazing sheep as we were.

Lunch at the Dewhursts was predictable:
a shepherd's pie, potatoes in their jackets
like hot stones mollified with knobs of butter,
a modicum of cider, little water,
followed by a huge baked apple each:
Saturn in a lake of steaming custard.

After another lecture about gun-safety,
we took our airguns into Oak Tree Wood
and talked about 12-bores and what we'd like,
the .303 and things I knew little about.
We searched for rabbits, rats and other vermin
to take a shot at,
boxes of pellets clicking in our trousers
like tiny pocket chessmen made of pewter.

Looking down the barrel
was a new pubertal thrill
a brass-lined spiral
to spin the exciting pellets
at high velocity towards their target.

There was a flutter in the bushes opposite.
We watched two little birds
making the noise of day.
Look, I said, and raised the air-rifle,

aligned the V-sight with the praying dot,
lifted the barrel to allow for gravity
and trusted to my practised inability
to hit the target.
I squeezed the trigger and split seconds later
a sparrow fell.
The other sparrow flew.
Their perch remained unmoved.

We sauntered over
and found my victim:
a hedge sparrow, all fluff
and tiny bones, with dangling feet,
now curled round nothing and the eyes half-shut.
We dropped him to become common as mud.
No burial in a pencil-box for him.

Then wandered off and I remember later
a skein of protected geese flying
high against a picture-postcard sunset,
a cirrus sky of litmus blue and pink,
above the Tamar estuary.
We took a pot-shot at the squadron V
and seconds later saw a wingspan move
and take evasive action.

High tea. Then home, returning in the dark.
The airgun parcelled up again
in corrugated cardboard and brown paper,
boy-tied and badly with string and hairy sisal.
The lane by lamplight
a terrifying gauntlet of high trees
between two woods,
the night and silence.

The bike-lamp making spectral shadows
with power of life and death.
The come-to-get-me shapes and noise of breathing.
The miles to cycle home in blind denial.

Combing the Beach

A stone, abraded and round,
pitted and white like the moon,

another the shape and size
of an almond sugared white,

a fragment of shell as smooth
and enamelled as a tooth,

hinge of a mussel shell
glinting with mother-of-pearl,

a broken nugget of quartz
scintillating with sparks,

slate in a tiny flake
and a piebald pebble for luck,

a shard of striated shell
still with a seafood smell,

a mollusc's auricular curve
echoing distant surf,

and a globe of luminous stone –
hold it towards the sun,

read the translucent veins
or lick the salt from the lens

to polish the colours afresh
before they evaporate

like life from the eye of a fish.

Breaking the Silence

The sea retaining day-heat into darkness,
The water surface glowed like beaten silver.
Hearing no waves but lapping at the shoreline,
I swam out at an angle to the moonlight,
My body not disturbing the reflections,
When suddenly from waters by my shoulder
Fish through the air went leaping after fish,
All in a silver arc above the surface.
Not frightened, though, exhilarated rather,
I let a little gasping sound escape
And thought they would not now repeat the blessing
Until again they jumped the silent water.
I felt a quivering sound behind my ear
And watched the arched perfection of the fish
Which leapt and entered with such quiet grace,
Unthreatened and unthreatening. No splashes.
A prayer and hallowed answer to a prayer.
If I could have the last rites here and now
That rainbow sacrament is what I'd choose:
My head anointed, swimming among swimmers,
A fluent road of moonlight to the skyline
And far above the oceanic moon.

Bougainvillaea

Why desire
to preserve forever
purple bougainvillaea
over turquoise sea,
not that the bluey-green
reflective aquamarine
is exactly turquoise
nor the balustrade of violet
purple in fact
or cobalt violet
and not flowers but bracts
over delicate florets
against a sunlit sea,
itself a fractured fluid
mirror of the sky's
nonentity?
Purple, mauve, violet,
it depends on the light
and idiolect
of the individual
viewing leaves as flowers
and, as Goethe
is said to have said,
even a sensitive person
can only look
at a sunset
for a limited time
or words to that effect.

BOMBYLANS

Sounds like a hornet or a wasp.
How can I tempt it to escape?
What does it see in a bathroom light
And lampshade with its star designs?
A sunflower stamen of hot moon
To energise and pollinate?

With rolled-up cosh of magazine
I try to lift the creature free.
It buzzes to the shade again
And hits the lightbulb with a ding.
Blinded by after-images
I stun it to the ground in fright

And glad it cannot testify
I club the living daylights out.
So was it just a hover fly
Or *volucella bombylans*,
A mimic of the bumble bee?
A samurai with Christian wings,

It had a bumble bee's low drone
And yellow with black tiger stripes
Its markings simulated wasp.
I hold it up to magnify
The Giant's Causeway of its eyes'
Bronze eyeballs in the stiffened corpse,

Dry, lightweight now. My breath can move
What seemed electric when alive.
In death so fragile it was love.

BEACHED

Like ancestors we decorate our caves
with images to make us feel at home.
The Chinese whispers of the little waves
issue their own obituaries in foam.

The powdered rock, the salt solution, air
where fronds and feather shapes of nebulous ice
on sunlit sky which is not anywhere
remind the writer nothing happens twice,

as through the hour-glass of each idle fist
I run the warm particulates of sand.
Time is a millstone and the body grist
to molecules of water, sky and land.

But where's the rationale, the *raison d'être*,
our universe has this or any feature?
Why do we lie here beached like injured creatures
unready to evolve into the future?

Looking for Driros

The Archaeological site of Malia
with its Minoan Palace was closed on Mondays.
So, tempted by the temple ideogram,
we thought we'd look again for Driros,
'a Dorian settlement with acropolis
and temple to Apollo Delphinios.'

We bought an orange each the size of grapefruit,
a juicy navel orange with the stem still in it
and skin fresh-smelling held against
the sky- and aqua-blues of the horizon
like a child's exemplar of the rising sun.
We saw a cockerel crowing by a lemon,
some purple-starred mesembryanthemums,
a coloured globe inside a village schoolroom
and read the local war memorial.
We heard the goat- and sheep-bells mix with birdsong
in herbal groves of oranges and olives
and looked at a Byzantine floor mosaic
of merry dolphins in an early church.

But could we find the turning-left for Driros?
We gave up somewhere in or near Kastelli,
neglecting now the road for Dories
and left the ruins for another day,
another stay or never.
Hard to discover what you come to find
on labyrinthine Crete or anywhere.

Instead at a hillside villa outside Fourni,
we saw improbably behind a fence
an ostrich standing by a prickly pear:
long-necked, arched eyebrows and bald cartoon head

expressing supercilious surprise,
it looked at us, then yawned, and yawned again,
its dowdy feather baggage of a body
perched on huge bony legs and two-toed feet.
A man on a donkey came the other way
and greeted us admirers of the ostrich,
as if it were now normal in his world
to see a flightless isolated bird,
one hatched from an enormous global egg
like Artemis, Apollo or the cosmos.

AUSPICE

Every ten years or so
I see or imagine I do
the bird I take for a sign,
a hoopoe (*Upupa epops*),
this last today on a pine
in Aghia Triada, Crete,
raising its crest and my hopes
of life in ruined remains
until it took sudden flight
to hide in another tree
(dazzling black and white wings
over improbable pinks)
and procreate in the mind
for another decade or three.

ARRIVALS

luggage rucksacks bags and labels
worldly goods on four-wheeled trolleys
floral skirts and stripy trousers
fancy shirt in papal purple
buzz-cuts ponytails and plaits
Toronto Stockholm Istanbul
blue shirts T-shirts patterned blouses
headphones earrings mobile phones
Indian silks with gilded threads
sari yashmak anorak
the toddlers and the aged crones
dark glasses worn on top of heads
the babes-in-arms and walking bones
a human river torrent flood
Karachi Calgary Bombay
old lady in white hat and gloves
New York Vancouver Port of Spain
all those passions dreams and loves
of mothers sisters fathers brothers
San Francisco San Diego
lovers and significant others
off to work or coming home
grimaces then the grins and smiles
of recognition after miles
mother of twins with double-buggy
wheelchair granny greeting children
immaculate Arab in white robe
rabbinical Jew in beard and hat
the orange Indian contingent
and look who's here flown all the way
from Melbourne Auckland and LA
mother daughter in embrace
family and familiar face

body smells of touch and taste
tears of reunited laughter
eyes of mother father daughter
like the travelled oceans water.

Arykanda

'That wall up there? That is the aqueduct
which took the water into Arykanda,
the same we pay for in those plastic bottles.
Come on, my friends, we're not in Britain now.
In Turkey, we buy fruit and eat. Enjoy
grapes, peaches, cherries, apricots and melon.

We're standing at the lowest level here
in the necropolis where we return.
For me this is most beautiful of sites
in whole of Asia Minor, my dear friends.
Walk up these steps to see the agora.
Imagine market place with busy shops,
a fountain in the middle where is olive,
the odeon where they discuss, and amphitheatre
for dramas when they worship Dionysus,
get drunk, forget themselves, do anything, make love.
All that is brutal in human nature found
expression here in Lycian Arykanda,
like sales of slaves and gladiator combat
as in the movie *Spartacus* with Kirk Douglas.
And here, dear friends, I smoke a cigarette
under a pine-tree while you can explore
the stadium on top of Arykanda.

So we return now to the temple-tombs.
Here is one of the earliest Christian symbols
on a sarcophagus. Chi-Rho for Christ
and alpha-omega for God Almighty.
And what's that face? A gorgon, yes, Medusa.
She turn you into stone if you are looking.

Winged Harpies lift the souls to afterlife
and once you're there you can't come back again.
Who wants reincarnation anyway?
And now to Elmali for lunch then mosque.'

Anubis and the Wet Nurse

Indoors, the rooms are painted white,
Even the floorboards. The furniture is metal.
My god-daughter is laughing as she shows me
The plates on the Edwardian dresser
Carved like a wooden altar: the linen starched,
The teacups, bowls and dishes neatly stacked,
White china, fluted casseroles,
In some of which pink gelatine has set
In sweet inedible membranes of taut jelly,
Too hard to be scooped up by spoon.
And have you nothing nutritive? I ask
But they laugh at the question.

The puppy in the bathroom lives
Inside a velvet pouch
With zipper and luxurious lining.
Permitted to look out in cushioned state,
His dog head is unzipped from time to time
When he is carried to the bathroom window.
He has your eyes, sad, brown and hungry.

His mother bares her eunuch dugs. No milk,
But fatty dumplings of blind mammaries
And so her swollen belly sprouts a penis.
They bring the puppy dog to suck on that
But I protest: 'It needs a mother's milk.'
So I am held and stripped down to the waist.
Bare-breasted, I must feed the dog-boy who
Both is and is not you.
I claw at both my breasts until they bleed.

Memento

Bearded Poseidon on the mantlepiece,
A photo of her father, Captain Mann,
Whose second daughter was Elizabeth,
The Universal Aunt to family,
Miss E.D.Mann, the grown-up who could play
Blow-football with us and Monopoly.

Great Auntie Betty showed us how to conjure
Brown woollen pompoms out of cardboard circles
And hollow swans from flattened silver paper,
Made holly berries out of sealing wax,
Taught us Clock Patience and then Spite and Malice,
Smoked Kensitas and harvested the coupons.

We loved her stories and her childish laughter:
'We gave him mousetrap cheese instead of soap.
He scrubbed and scrubbed and still it wouldn't lather.'
Outback on evenings in Australia,
She'd learnt to smoke to fumigate mosquitoes.
Her hoopla'd smoke rings wobbled like a signal.

Now when I think of Auntie B I hear
The bleeping of a deaf-aid maladjusted,
The clinking shopping bags of Cyprus sherry,
I see a dogged hook-nosed hen in glasses
And endless games of two-pack patience stalled
In feudal columns on a wooden tray.

She wrote my name in loopy handwriting
And added for inscription on the card:
'My badge worn all through First World War in France
Queen Alexandra's Imperial Nursing Sisters'
And safety-pinned the ribbon to the paper.
I keep the keepsake like a talisman.

The flat. The room. The nursing home. The coffin.
The girl. The nurse. The aunt. The Great Aunt Betty
Who has no bronze memorial but this.
I see you arriving somewhere on a ship
Met at a quayside by the bearded man.
It is an anchorage and you embrace.

Auntie Millie

Who or what was
Auntie Millie?

Whose half-sister
and whose aunt?

To what extent
was she family?

And was she really
Millicent or Emily?

Where is her likeness
or facsimile?

And do I remember her
vaguely, dimly?

Did she like Pelmanism
and red anemones?

In what kind of home
was she resident?

Did she sit in a dayroom
grimly, dreamily

in the asylum
of her senility?

What did she make
of the man from Galilee?

What was her singular
gift or ability?

And is this homily
or lament

for Great Aunt Millie,
maiden aunt,

anomaly
or nonevent?

Niagara

I salute you, O Frenchman, fellow-republican,
Crosser of chasms, traverser of rivers,
Walking on a rope of hempen fiber
Above the roaring thunder of mighty Niagara.

A human miracle over a natural wonder,
You walk step by step on the tautened rope
Above the spume, the spray, the ever-rising vapor
Of the cataract's incessantly tumbling torrent.

On a filament, balanced between America and Canada,
You perform mid-crossing an impudent somersault
Over a cumulus cloud of spray-water rising.

Small man with balancing-pole, in circus costume,
You wear a blindfold and saunter over the abyss
In the watery smells of the misty air.

You cannot hear the shouts and cheers of the thousands
Watching your nimble footwork over precipitous vistas,
As we applaud the magnitude of your achievements
Above the magnificent drop of the roaring waters.

O Blondin, bridger of chasms,
I extol your unique intrepidity
As I salute Niagara afresh in this song.

The torrent unabashed, unabated, rushes headlong to crash
Into the tumult of the diluvian waterfall,
A half-drowned rainbow spectral in all that spray.

Above it you walk on a tightrope and all the while
Blue Ontario moves towards Erie
Over mighty Niagara falling, night and day.

Ghost Town

We crush the rock in a simple mill
Powered by water and by mule.

A section of the mine caves in
Exposing a rich gold-bearing vein.

They pay the girls in the saloons
Who bare their bartered flesh and bones.

I preach the gospel's temperance
To gambling halls and opium dens.

To us the pinyon pine is sacred,
Its protein nuts a winter secret.

We are the Paiute Indians
Watching the slaughter of our pines.

These are the mountains where they mine
The silver dollar of the moon,

The golden pollens of the sun
From subterranean metal shine.

A silver blizzard overland
Buries the miners underground

Between the veins of sunken gold,
Gleaned as the naked globe congealed.

Open 365 Days

With a cough of steam
it seems to come
almost on time

from its under-
ground chamber
smelling of sulphur,

a sudden eruption
from souterrain
onto the scene,

a nebulous feather
of hot white water
and steam under pressure,

both genie and ghost,
a hothouse growth
of miraculous birth

for less than a minute
splashes the intimate
flesh of the planet

until it relapses
onto the plateaux
of its own applause.

On bamboo and grass
hot droplets glitter
like dew or stars.

At Pismo Beach

The heads bob up and down like marker-buoys
revealing company of seals at sunset,
swimming and diving out beyond the pier.
The sky's a flight-path for the pelicans
returning to their guano-covered rocks.
We eat some cherries and ripe mango each
for which the salesman had a special name,
a fruit that ripens central to the grove
with quintessential sweetness round the stone.
The surfers catch the last big waves of daylight
while men lure fish dusk-feeding off the pier,
whose wooden bridge leads nowhere out to sea.
The royal road of sunlight to the mountains
ignites the water till the day is night.

Pacific

The roving eye of my typhoon
Will smash your flimsy dwellings down.

So what's your Christian name for me,
The hurricane still out to sea?

Through Frisco and Los Angeles,
Grinding the rock, I shift and squeeze:

I am the San Andreas Fault
In waiting for the next assault.

When Mount St Helens woke from sleep
And blew her grey volcanic slope,

I felled a redwood forest flat,
Buried the masts and drowned the fleet.

We are tsunami in the dark
Who navigate the aftershock

Then break on the Pacific rim
To see how far the land can swim.

I am the Mindanao Trench
Plotting a mountainous revenge

On all the slimy untermensch
Who fill my underwater range.

I am the moon's unflowering stone,
I bear my scarface, cold, alone,

Pulling the blanket side to side
To stimulate the ocean tide.

But when we saw the mushroom cloud
Some felt afraid and others proud

That such a race of vermin could
Irradiate its own abode.

Petrified Forest

Next to a living stand of Douglas Fir,
We touch the redwood like an ancestor.

It is a sculpture in its sepulchre.
The clothes of resurrection do not stir.

San Francisco Bay

On the foreshore at Sausalito,
a suntanned fisherman,
balding with hairy back,
is reeling in a catch.

The curved antenna of his rod and line
has drawn a crowd who gasp
when what breaks surface is a ray:
sad cartoon eyes and Moomin mouth,
its underbelly moon-white as a sail.

And as a colleague cuts the barb
free from the suffocating pout,
the twitchy aerial of tail
overarcs its back and writhes.

The fisherman uplifts it by the gills
for all to see and photograph,
then lobs it back and with a splash
the belly-flopping ray
has undulated out of sight again
into the thought of San Francisco Bay.

Agave Americana

I am standing again at the North Rim
looking towards the mantle of the earth.
So this is a cross-section of the crust,
the sedimentary ledges, cliffs and slopes,
the light-reflecting rock and canyon trees,
the blank horizon Arizona blue.

We come to worship a gigantic gorge
and sublimate our human pettiness
inside an introverted mountain range,
as if we could like eagles soar above
the rock formations and their tyrant stare
with consecrated and Wagnerian names.

These rocks here at the top, a bird's eye view,
were once the bottom of an inland sea,
from which we gaze on distant birds and tree-tops
of ponderosa pine and juniper,
as mesas, buttes and precipices are
repainted by the sunrise and the sunset.

I come here once again in troubled mind
to transcend petty insignificance,
my own and other people's, to assuage
the anonymity of hopelessness
and watch the flowering of the century plant
whose plume is pliant in the canyon wind.

America

We changed the tyre, we changed the wheel,
approached the thing with vim and zeal,
we bathed the parts in motor oil,
we took the auto to the wash
and sprayed it with a pressure hose,
we tried denial, tried to josh,
oh shit, we said, but shit smelt better
than this excremental foetor.
We went berserk with lemon juice,
we tried to turn the demon loose
and exorcise its stinking ghost.
Grease monkeys underneath the chassis
from Frisco Bay to Tallahassee,
we tried the lot from fruit to louche,
from ketchup to vaginal douche,
in car parks right across the States,
detergents, sprays and sublimates,
deodorants, deodorizers,
atom bombs and atomizers,
but could we rid it of the rank
offending stench of reeking skunk?
We learnt to dread the vehicle
as if it owned the pungent smell,
as if the murder was our meal
and we were in a kind of hell.
The car keys and upholstery
began to stink of yesterday.
A creature walking in the road
had heard its skin and bone explode
and in its death throes it had squirted
skunk-spray at the thing which hurt it.
The car became a coffin where
we decomposed and breathed the air.

A Better Berry

*'Doubtless God could have made a better berry,
but doubtless God never did.'*
              Dr Boteler quoted by Izaak Walton

Reach down between the green serrated groves
And feel for berries' ripened crimson selves
Wearing their seeds like buttons on a sofa,

Twiddle the six-point star of Bethlehem
Between your pink forefinger and your thumb
To reinvent the wheel with leaf and stem,

Then with some Amaretto – just a splash –
Taste at its best, sun-ripened and picked fresh,
The veiny brainwork of the sweetened flesh

With caster sugar crystals by the spoonful
And cream poured in a languid waterfall
Onto the waiting strawberries in a bowl,

Then savour both the shape in the saliva
And that infallible midsummer flavour
As if you were in love and it your lover,

Moving the proof from lips to uvula
And swallow, swallow till the fever's over,
As if in heaven and an unbeliever.

Spring

Two pigeons sit
or perch of an evening
on the blank street-light
before it illumines,
orange in blue:
one sits unmoving,
the other one fidgets
with headtalk and beak
caressing the neck
till, with a dove-grey
shaking of feathers,
Winged Victory
hops up and flutters
over his peace dove,
making the metalwork
shake like a stem
woken and suddenly
vibrant with spring.

Seed

The juice inside the hollow stem
of dandelion milk
feeds florid sun to faded moon
and dandelion all too soon
becomes a dandelion clock
releasing on the breeze to breed
each tiny parachutist seed
which leaves a mini pockmarked dot
whereon each single-minded foot
premeditated flight.
The race in May to be September
is paradise on earth and yet
the seeds which never knew remember
and we remember to forget.

A Burnt Out Case

I

Was it intolerable to leave behind
The island Crete, its wine-soaked fishermen,
Their peasant pettiness a symbol of
The whole parochial pellet known as Earth,
Its planetary moonshine like a mirror
Glimpsed in the night, no vanities to reflect?

Was it for pride I wanted to explore
The aboriginal archipelagoes
Of fiery islands in their vault of silence?
And to rename as if at Genesis
The antique statuary of constellations:
Shadrak and Meshak in the Fiery Furnace.

II

And then for one short instant I became
Starlight myself and supernova flame.

Look at my body charcoaled by the sun,
A corpse's shadow and a lightning burn.

That is my heart, that lump of sealing-wax,
Which sets the seal on all your mortal works.

Against a backdrop of an ocean sky,
Ultramarine though neither night nor day

The anti-aircraft shellbursts of my dream
Echo inside the cold continuum.

Appointment

The Hypnotherapy Centre
is offering expert help with
depression anxiety
confidence relaxation
meditation sleeping
slimming smoking
phobias sex problems
studying/exams
bedwetting goals
drive test nail biting
hay fever bust improvement
worrying loneliness
concentration memory
jealousy drinking
problem behaviour
nerves migraine
acne cystitis
peace of mind
happy childbirth
self hypnosis
marital problems
spiritual development
telepathy ESP
lucid dreaming
astral projection
creative thinking
slowing ageing.
Doesn't that make you feel
better already?

The Shade of Sir John Betjeman Revisits Bletchley, Bucks.

'From Wolverton to Woburn Sands,
It reproduces and expands
While roundabouts and ring-roads breed
The signs which baffle cars at speed.

Where are the villages and farms
Instead of air-conditioned palms?
Where are the cows that used to graze
On fields devoured by motorways?

If only planners of the whole
Could practise urban birth control,
Or if they had some civic pride
Could volunteer for suicide.

Reject the tarmac and the florist,
Return to wildflowers in the forest,
Give back the bricks to river clay
And speed the process of decay.

Let every artificial lake
Admit it is a damp mistake,
Let denizens of planner's blight
Evacuate it overnight.

Come back, Polaris submarines,
And redirect your war machines,
O Milton's God at Milton Keynes
And smash the place to smithereens.'

No Time Wasters Please

Hoity-toity
Widow Twankey
Maydays toyboys
Hanky-panky.

Leo *con brio*
Inveigles Virgo
For rookie nookie
Hookey *a tergo*.

Miguel (Chigwell)
District/Central
Seeks oriental
Genital rental.

Arty party
Longs to be smitten
By pretty witty
Titty kitten.

Rugger-bugger,
Meathead, tight-head,
Needs dotty totty
Naughty-nightied.

Giddy biddy
Feisty, faddy,
Craves fuddy-duddy
Sugar Daddy.

Italian stallion
Tutti-frutti
Fancies chances
Black beauty.

Lavish McTavish
Clean shaven,
Wants foreign sporran,
Raven haven.

Randy dandy
Hung like hummingbird
Seeks bimbo Bambi
Far from herd.

Bounty hunter,
Home Counties,
Grim Reaper
Hunts bounties.

Sometimes

Sometimes I want to scream,
Sometimes I long to yell
And utter a censorless stream
Of consciousness in hell.

Sometimes I want to rebel,
Sometimes I want to scrawl
As if in a prison-cell
Graffiti on the wall.

Sometimes I long to breed
Without being too well-bred
To scatter the carefree seed
Like a dandelion head.

Sometimes I pray for a creed,
Belief in myself as well,
And sometimes the heart does bleed,
Not that the bleeders can tell.

Sometimes I want to keen
My grievances and grief
Like a tragic heroine
Without the comic relief.

Sometimes I wish I had said
Yes I'm completely to blame.
Sometimes I wish I were dead
And others would wish the same.

Sometimes I'm close to the brink,
Sometimes it's further on down
But often I wish I could sink
In the waters of life and drown.

Song of Innocence and Inexperience

While Diffidence thought Arrogance
Inordinately proud,
Arrogance called Diffidence
Simperingly cowed.

Diffidence with a carving knife
Hid by the garden shed,
Fought Arrogance and then himself
Until the bushes bled.

Thus innocent and experienced,
Those twins of self-regard,
Young Arrogance and Diffidence
Died in their own back yard.

Impasse

You are the victim,
I am to blame.
You eat my pride,
I drink your shame.

You are the mother
To my child.
We think each other
Infantile.

I am the stranger
To your pain.
You are the anger
In my brain.

I use the silence,
You the pause.
You are the martyr,
I the cause.

Insomnia

Your mentors and tormentors join
in the small hours to toss a coin
the coin is you and heads or tails
whichever choice it always fails
call for the bottle narcotize
with television sex food lies
another addled egghead cracked
inside the factory of fact
where dawn attacks with blacks and blues
the sunset is a psychic bruise
and night and day land sky and sea
are solipsists like you and me
so sleep on it and wake up worse
call for a psychiatric nurse
delete the fate you cannot face
also-ran in a one-horse race
and what you have is what you've got
from cancer ward to carrycot
but what is that you nenuphar
floating lily or drowning star
it's all too little and too late
to hibernate or aestivate
so scrub the future shred the past
as overcrowded overcast
if things are never what they seem
it's only an anxiety dream

Nature of the Art

Poems are anti-depressants –
They're better than booze or pills.
Buy two or three books as presents
And say goodbye to your ills.

Poets are never depressives.
They always and promptly pay bills.
They're never offensive obsessives.
It's life and life only that kills.

Inconsequence

Beneath case history
artistry casuistry

below *donnée* and data
human and nature

behind the admirer
immured in the mirror

beyond wind's signature
mountain and water

after the aftermaths
mysteries myths

under the enmity
envying envy

without the rancour
counselling anger

outside the insular
cellar and solar

let the identity
free of self-pity

wish and fulfilment
failure defilement

re-enter oblivion's
impervious silence

Origin of the Species

What possessed the fish to creep
Onto mudflats from the deep?
Who rehearsed the ape to stand,
Weapons fashioned in its hand?

What made simian physique
Simulate and then to speak?
How and why did cultured ape
Outlaw incest, war and rape?

In what oceans of whose mind
Was the human form designed?
What short circuit of whose brain
Flicks the human switch insane?

What creation or creator
Improvised the detonator?
Who divined the seen unseeing
To bemuse the human being?

Why enmesh the turning earth
In the cords of human birth?
What engendered spume and spark
In the ampoule of the dark?

Shark

Did the shark produce within
Rasping notions of its skin?
Was it chance or by design
Fin departed from the spine?

Off what continental shelf
In the current of itself
Did the shark devise its smirk,
Sudden bite and savage jerk?

Who is what when sharks attack
Solo or in hunting pack,
Panicking at bleeding flesh
Frenzied fish and mammal creche?

Breathing meditated kills
Through the slashes of its gills,
In what underwater shrine
Does it worship blood in brine?

In what Nazareth of youth
Fed the bone that bred the tooth?
In what Bethlehem was born
Ocean tiger's dorsal thorn?

Snakes and Meteors

A stone's throw from the human race
along an ancient forest track,
below the leaf mould in the dark,
there is a buried edifice.
It smells of human sacrifice
of alcohol and fractured skull,
not far from where a watercourse
is irrigating roots and moss.

Draw back the gates of undergrowth,
scoop out the greenery and earth,
polish with spit the muddy slime
and soon the fragments start to gleam:
though made of tiny tesserae
like polychromatic butterflies
above a field of fragrances,
the sullied blue is daylight sky.

Here is both recipe and meal
which offers dance and ritual:
the maenads and a minotaur
with Corybants in silence yell,
then feast on lobster, feed on boar.
Are those the spirals of the sea
with arms and legs like octopi?
Or are they snakes and meteors?

Here on a ley line is a node
of numinous beatitude
where time is free to concentrate
in the concentric rings of thought
plying the waters of the mind

as from a pebble in a pond
or growth rings in a giant wood
to ponder living and beyond.

To stare too long at this device
which is like birdsong fossilized
can lead to madness and despair.
There is a gorgon and its gaze
can petrify the worshipper
as priests of anger disappear
on quests for lapidary freaks
like statues in the River Styx.

There is no guarantee once found
that you will trace the wood again.
You may not trespass or possess.
Replace the greenery and earth,
put back the gates of undergrowth,
return along the pilgrim path
and fill a bottle from the source.
For which give thanks. Redeem. And bless.

Two Tigers

He snarls revealing ancestry of sabre tooth,
the epic force and delicacy
of tomcat gangster and his feline moll
turning from predator
to sentimental.

It is a sex-show and a ritual,
the instant nudity of fur on fur,
such intricate expertise.

Before Africa and India
parted company
and left the ocean
holding Madagascar,
their Asian camouflage was designed
by forest and savannah.

The unity of stripe on stripe
of charcoal shadow
on tawny sunlight listens to the noise:
the guttural growl of prehistoric rapture,
the molten heat of magma in the mantle
erupting volcanically into tiger ecstasy,
a foreign cry of ululated joy,

engendering of tiger on a tiger,
in a lineage stretching back
before the Ice Ages
into the living meat of Eocene.

Like a ribcage painted on,
a skeletal pattern of leaf shadow stripes,
the dark bars on its pelt

contain no prisoner or pilgrim,
the black stripes of its uniform
no criminal but
footpad and talon
of naked perfection.

In the acrobatic cat-show circus smells,
it is a double act of cat on cat
to replicate cat synergy
and propagate the progeny
of *Panthera tigris*,
tiger on tigress ab origine.

He theatrical at full throttle,
she fighting with her pelvis for survival
under the Rocky Mountains of his spine.
Watch the tension of sinew and bone
on muscle and skin.
The musical lashings of tail.
The whites of the eyes and bloodshot
numinous visions of insemination
as hindlegs devour each other
with only a mouth and tongue
and loins surrender
to a mind of their own.

The bared pink gum and calcified knife
of bone-dagger tooth
hovers an emblem above
the semblance of a satiable smile
between white whiskers of the female,
as he plants ejaculate
deep in the womb's throat
for ovary and sperm
to perform their version of the same

microcosmic moondance copulation
like salmon homing
up the darkened stream to spawn.

Soon she will roll over to reveal
dark nipples nestling in white belly fur.
He will drink for five minutes or more
quantities of water as after a kill
like a cat lapping milk from a saucer.

Vision Mixer

Abracadabra. Magic wand.
Please read my thought waves and respond.

You know my number. Ring me now.
Surprise yourself and break a vow.

Distressed, possessed, *id est* obsessed,
I have this passionate request.

I want you now. I want you here.
I want you in my egosphere.

I'm willing you to drive this way.
Telepathy. I hope and pray.

Drop everything. Get in the car.
Accelerate. Come as you are.

Without you time goes oh so slow
North of despair and east of woe.

Tonight began more years ago
Than I would ever let you know.

Zoological Gardens

Anti-clockwise round and round
the oval concrete pond,
he paces with both eyes half-closed,
ears flapping back and forwards with each step.
The tubular prehensile snout
uncurls to sniff and suck between
the giant toenails of his round front feet.

She meanwhile strips a branch of leaves
and lunches off them.
She's swaying rhythmically
as if she had in mind
some melody or dance.

He snorts a scoop of gravel
and spray-dusts his back,
picks up an apple bobbing green in water
and places it inside his whiskered mouth
between discoloured and uneven tusks.

Shifting methodically from foot to foot,
she pulls and chews more greenery.

And as he passes on his rounds,
the trunk sniff-feels for her until
another large proboscis gradually appears.
The human adults joke and snigger as,
preoccupied and ponderous, he paces round,
a naked prisoner at exercise,
then tries to mount her, fails, and tries again.
Men, women, children gather, shouting, laughing,
a circus crowd as for a circus act:
two Asian elephants in Melbourne Zoo.

She turns and raises by its muscled root
her fly-whisk tail,
and slowly, gently wades into the water
until knee-deep
to help him mount and couple with her,
though not for long, and afterwards,
protuberance retreating into pouch,
the bull continues on his rounds again.
Impassively, she turns her back on us
and briskly drops
three neatly-formed and ochre turds
into the drinking water where they float
and then she urinates
to human protestations of disgust
as if instinctual desires writ large
were both inhuman and preposterous.

Sunday at Messanges Plage

Between pine forest and Atlantic surf
Along the fallow avenue of sand,
Sun-worshippers prostrate anointed selves
To feel the warmth on shoulderblades and spine
And roast the pigmentation of the skin.
The Landes Coast beaches welcome naturists:
An Aryan Adam and Eve with an Alsatian
In their pretence of Paradise on Earth,
A stockbroker's Tahiti of the mind,
Where beach umbrellas sport their primary colours
And whistle-blowing lifeguards watch for danger.
Closed eyes reduce the beach to sounds and smells:
A bat-and-ball game, coconut suntan oil,
French, Dutch and German family languages.
Those tribal wars of Europe may be over
And yet a slit-eyed pillbox guards the beach,
A hoplite's helmet and a cenotaph
For Cockleshell heroes of another era.
Each sunlit breaker with a reef of spray
Collapses in an avalanche of foam
Onto the milled millennia of the sand,
Whose powdered surface emulates the moon's,
Itself a cloud now in a cloudless sky
And so remote it's difficult to believe
That such a delicate half communion wafer
Could motivate vast tonnages of water
In all the starlit emptiness of space,
The stars themselves meanwhile invisible.

The Great Pirarucu

Earth has many wonders
but few so wonderful as woman
who has a sense of humour and of numen
who shares her monthly cycle with the moon
who can see through the transparencies of men
who gives her body's lodgings to another
who can clear up the vomit blood and faeces
who can hear the endearments and decode the motives
who can outlive marriages husbands widowhood.

Earth has many other wonders, admittedly,
including that fish in the Amazon,
one of the largest freshwater fish,
the great antique Pirarucu.
Up to three metres long,
it weighs half a ton,
has teeth on its tongue
and its only predator is man.

Thesaurus

Fingerprints with loops and arches
Form inside the mother's womb.
Whorls define the thumbs and fingers
Before the body has a name.

The teacher in her classroom teaches
Children, pencils, fingers, thumbs
How to trace the shapes of letters
And figures representing sums.

Surnames schooled but not as orphans
In an idiom far from home
Are taught the languages of wolf-cubs
Modern France and Ancient Rome.

From Indo-Europeans, Greeks,
Declensions and infinitives,
Through us the native language speaks
Its rivers of derivatives.

And words arrive from every angle:
Sounds and signs, profound, profane,
The futuristic and old-fangled
Compose the lexis of the brain

Until the shadow of a dream
Is over and a pile of bones
Commemorates the primal scream
Whose lake of dreams is like the moon's.

Thought

Let dogmatic churchmen bind
religion to a cross,
let politicians try to blind
a people to its loss,

they can't incarcerate a mind
inside the edifice
or re-elect although resigned
another populace.

Hong Kong Island

A U.S. commando
(batteries included)
crawls on the tarmac
in combat gear.

A tiger-striped lobster
is trying to clamber
out of trapped seawater
onto the pier.

On a glazed footbridge
a beggar on cardboard
moves without moving,
a crippled pariah.

Characters in chalk
caption his story.
Coins beg for coins.
Hands claw in prayer.

As if he were lying
dead and invisible,
people pass by him
like water or air.

A Million Licensed Guns

The Godfrey family's picnicking
Below the summer trees.
Mother, son and daughter
See a gunman and they freeze.
The thirteen shots ring out
And birds fly in the air.
He stops to get some petrol,
Fills his Vauxhall car,
Then like they do in hold-ups,
Like they do in films,
He terrifies with gunshots
The girl behind the till.

It's a sunny Wednesday
In a Berkshire market town.
Paraffin flames are burning
His terrace to the ground.
And seeing in his garden
Mr Abdul Khan,
Michael Ryan shoots him
As he motor-mows the lawn.
He shoots because they think him
Lovable and soft
The mother who adored him
And the labrador he loved.

So Mrs Ryan's lying
In a roadside pool of blood
And slumped inside his squad car
PC Brereton is dead.
Marcus Barnard's taxi
Isn't going far –
A bullet through the windscreen's

His final taxi-fare,
And Francis Butler, wounded,
Is dying on a path
Leading to the gardens
Round the local cenotaph.

Hearing things, Ken Clements thinks
It's only kids at play.
His wife and family watch him
Fall for Rambo's toy.
The bullets come from Hungary,
The weapon is Chinese –
It's semi-automatic,
Like the licensee
Who's holed up in a classroom
In a comprehensive school.
He's got one bullet left now
But the trigger's hard to pull.

There's silence from the classroom
And then a muffled thud.
And in the town of Hungerford,
There's sixteen people dead.

United Nations

A present
from the Kenyan and
Zimbabwe governments,
an enormous life-size
bull elephant,
cast in bronze,
has been donated
to the United Nations.

The sculptor made a mould
of the elephant
and reproduced the creases
in the epidermis
of the aged pachyderm.
But then what an absurd
international crisis
has occurred!

It had an erection
under anaesthetic.
The Secretary General
has been to look
and has decreed
the offending member
need not be gelded
nor truncated by a plumber.

Shrubbery will hide
the rubbery long prong
of totem normally tucked
discreetly into scrotum

till arse-high elephant grass
can be planted to disguise
its mammoth martyrdom
and make it feel at home.

So there it stands,
blind monument
to impotence
and anaesthesia
with swollen glans.

Wild West

The evidence
in a court of law
would not convict
so let's to war.

Too much too soon
is not too late
to reunite
the United States.

Son of a bitch
son of a gun
better decide
which side you're on.

Man with a mandate
land of the free
I gotta date
with destiny.

I tell you straight
I'm a loving guy
but those we hate
is gonna die.

He hits and runs
he shoots and kills
he hides in holes
he hides in hills.

Mood of the people's
tough and mean.
Nobody cripples
our war machine.

We'll teach the shitty
infidel
to bomb our city
and burn in hell.

After the Sermon

A modest audience assembles
In the Pillar Room for Geoffrey Hill,
Billed as the last great Modernist,
On whose King Penguin Gauguin cover
A Jacob wrestles with an angel.
Enter Hill in a charcoal suit,
Ascetic, clerical, academic,
Socks a Bohemian Fauvist mauve,
He stands up to enunciate
With minimal proselytising prose
His terse hermetic po-faced runes
Intoned in donnish monotones.

In the Main Hall meanwhile, what's that?
Children. Rats. Pied Piper. Feet
And gales of interruptive laughter.
Is Cheltenham Spa Hamelin on heat?
No, boys and girls greet Postman Pat,
An actor in a postman's hat
And specially converted van,
Who's come to entertain his fans,
While Geoffrey Hill looks faintly pained
As at an agonising pun
To hear his verbal music stained
By unpremeditated fun.

Best Before End

dot dot dot the future
stop full stop the past
there's no dot like the present
and dash it will not last.

Bloodsucker

Baring my buttocks, I've been bitten to buggery.
My midriff is measled by midge or mosquito,
Twenty-two, twenty-three tumps on the torso
From hipbone to hambone, ankle to abdomen,
Itchy as an irritant, scratchy as an allergy.

Jumping on the bandwagon of my underpants,
It must have hurrahed in my hairier areas,
Raising with its rasula monuments to menus
Of blood group, body soup, corpuscle and muscle juice.
It even pricked my pecker for its prandial peccadilloes.

Come out, little parasite, wherever you are:
You are my blood-brother or his sozzled sister.
I bet you are bilingual in Malaria and English.
I want to shake you by the end of an antenna
And squeeze your bloody body till it bursts like a polyp.

Chapter One

A psychosexual melodrama
With bit parts for the Dalai Lama,
Concorde, aerobics, Montezuma,
Samantha Fox and the Bodmin Puma,
It will be published in Swahili,
Blessed by the Pope and Dennis Healey,
Top the bestsellers and its stars
Will osculate their Oscar's arse.
A chandelier from a golden age,
Its wit will sparkle from the page;
The prose style will seduce apostles,
Inspire a cult and critical gospels.

Today I am going to start the novel
Which will render evil for evil
And embitter my bitterest rival.
Mythopoeic like Eve and the apple,
The snake will have sex and sex appeal.
Its hero, Hugh, and villain, Hugo,
(Me and my alter ego's ego)
Will thicken the plot and hit the bottle;
The ballet in metal turns into a battle
And the ogre's killed in Castle Drogo.
Today and tomorrow I shall write reams.
All I am stuck for is a title.
Would *Dreams of Conquest, Conquest of Dreams*
Both be unsaleable and unsubtle?

Equal Opportunism

My personal computer is politically correct:
It agrees with E.M.Forster that if only we connect
The world would be much better for electors and elect.
It's been to universities and as you might expect
Has honorary doctorates and dozens to collect.
It's party apolitical and wholly circumspect:
With a reading age of 50 and a Mensa intellect,
It scans the Sunday papers and it never could neglect
The poor of any country – it can e-mail them direct.
Where bigotry's obligatory, it's certain to reject
The sexist or sectarian of either sex or sect.
With its unbiased judgement it would never deselect
The redhead or the dreadlocked, the freckled or the flecked.
Its spelling is as spelling goes impeccably well checked,
So clean in thought and verbiage it could never interject
A blasphemous excretive or words to that effect.
It's read the works of Kipling and *Collected Plays* of Brecht
And when it speaks in German, the Deutsch is ultra *echt*.
It doesn't smoke, it never drinks, nor fornicates erect.
It wears no prophylactics having nothing to protect,
No intravenous penis and nothing to inject.
It's not a phallic symbol and no hen has ever pecked
Its status or equipment which you're welcome to inspect:
It's taken twenty centuries to patent and perfect.
It's genuinely neuter and one of the select,
Both confidant(e) and tutor, though as it may suspect,
Because my libidego has a chauvinist effect,
My personal correctness is politically wrecked.

Common or Garden

In the late spring or early summer
The conjugants approach each other
In darkness at a snail's pace
For footsy-footsy, face-to-face.

Anterior tentacles elongate,
Quiver and bend to touch a mate
Till after fifteen minutes or so
Of staying in contact toe-to-toe

Hermaphrodisiac half-inch darts
Impart to partners' private parts
The strange calcareous shaft of Venus
Which stimulates in each a penis

And when they've coupled for hours and hours
With scant regard for plants or flowers,
Then *exeunt* on a moonlit trail,
A pregnant from a pregnant snail.

Neighbourhood Watch

Pretty woman walks to wood.
High heels and fishnet tights.
What's she doing? Can't be good.
Net curtains twitch aside.
Lipstick and cigarette.
Wiggle bottom, jiggle tits.
Who's she going to meet?
Daily doilies can't decide.
Recognise her? No, not yet.
Tarty slut. Outdoors. Tut, tut.

Sleazy geezer leaves the wood.
Where's he left her? Makes you sick.
What if her assaulted nude's
Bleeding in the bluebell wood?
Voice suspicion. 999.
Help. Murder. Rapist. Crime.
Hurry. Woman victim. Quick.
Ambulance. The nick of time.
Police arrive and make arrest:
Transvestite and his party dress.

Not Today

Five o'clock dawn
birdsong twilight
six o'clock snooze
delay delight
seven dream on
till eight o'clock
and traffic noise
stretch out the arm
then 999
alarm alarm
it's half past yawn
get up get up
five more minutes
half-past ten
then it's then it's
failed again
promise self
to get up soon
struggle deeper
after noon
hot-backed sleeper
trains of thought
carrying freight
frightened fraught
under the duvet's
mope and moulder
eyelid movies
simmer smoulder
procrastinator
swear a vow
later later
no not now
when I'm older

wiser better
I Canute
with feet of clay
will face the waves
but not today.

Target

When I was on my way to teach
One Saturday in shirt-sleeve order,
A pigeon in a copper beech
Admiring a herbaceous border,
A bottom-heavy type of bird,
A winged and feathered tub of lard
With an intestinal disorder,
Released a liquid pigeon turd.

What had it eaten? Dread to think.
What puddles had it had to drink?
At least it missed the balding head
And hit the shoulder blade instead,
Thus staining shirt of Virgin blue
With guano splat of pigeon poo,
An epaulette of khaki-white
And evil-smelling pigeon-shite.

So shirtily that Saturday,
'I have been shat upon,' I say.
The swollen yahoo of a bird
Less gastroenteritic turd
Feels meanwhile lightened of its load
And like a levitating toad
It takes off through the branches to
A sky of unsuspecting blue.

Tears

The vision starts to liquefy
And lower lip to tremble,
The voice begins to thicken
And features to resemble
The back end of plucked chicken,
As infant breathing fills the lungs
To prime the bawling treble yell,
The face and body puce as tongues,
Blood beating at the fontanelle,
And baby face begins to cry
So many different kinds of tears.

The tears distilled into a sonnet,
The tears of grief held back for years,
Tears of frustration, tears of rage,
Tears of if-all-the-world's-a-stage
Why aren't I honoured on it.
Tears that taste of swallowed pride
Or chateau-bottled suicide,
The mimed boohoo behind the hands,
The true secretion of the glands
That taste of tears, those saline drips
Directed by the tongue to lips,
The tears that stain the pillowslip
And weep the sorry self to sleep.

The orchestra of misery
Is such a universal plea
I find it idle to believe
That only *homo sapiens* cries
To vent its grievances and grieve.
So blow your nose and dry your eyes,
Hold out your hand for a surprise,

While I remember those that I
Deliberately have caused to cry
And hope that they forgive me my
Predisposition to deny
That Jesus wept and so have I.

Downing Street Cat

I am the next Messiah and New Labour's on a roll,
We're capturing the centre at a steady Gallup poll,
My policies are pragmatist, my principles a blur:
Consensus and democracy are words that make me purr.
My record's *rasa tabula* but razor-sharp my claws,
I am a wily bureaucat who speaks without a pause.

> With permosmile and pressure chat,
> I'm grinning like the Cheshire cat,
> A cat that gets the cream.
> I practise in the mirror
> Both looking grim and trimmer,
> The winning smile, my wily guile,
> The frank, déclassé, candid style
> Which will perfect the dream.

I've never been a minister or high in public office
But there is nothing sinister in voting for a novice;
I want to catch the early worm inside the Tory bird
And redesign the kingdom before King Charles III.
My pedigree is variegate, I am a mongrel moggie,
My brain is full of northern grit, my words are southern-soggy.

> An Old Fettesian orator,
> I look like an ex-chorister
> With growing hopes of fame.
> No dope-head nor draft dodger,
> I neither grope nor roger
> Except one married barrister –
> To name her could embarrass her
> But Cherie is her name.

I promise you grand promises, I promise you no sleaze,
I am a lovely family man and desperate to appease.
I represent the Mansion House, I represent the masses
And I can play at cat and mouse with Fascists of all classes.
I brandish my bland blandishments on every telly channel
And blind with my embellishments Establishment grey flannel.

    A St John's Oxford graduate,
    So passionately moderate
    My honorary doctorate
    Could come from anywhere –
    So long as the electorate,
    The blessèd British plebiscite,
    Elects for its Protectorate
    The blessèd Tony Blair.

                (1997)

Euroland

(to be sung to the tune of the National Anthem by massed choirs in whatever accents seem appropriate)

> Good Europeans we
> Embrace our destiny
> For better life.
> Sink all our differences
> Under trade surpluses,
> Forget our histories
> Of war and strife.
>
> Under the CAP
> Let us remember we
> Are what we eat:
> Genetically modified
> Sprayed and emulsified
> Subsidized certified
> Butter and wheat.
>
> Let the good eurocrat
> And fellow diplomat
> Justify ends:
> Happy the federalist
> Non-controversialist,
> Come and be Judas-kissed
> Now we are friends.
>
> God save the gravy-train,
> Strasbourg and back again,
> God save our seat.
> Excess bureaucracy
> Brussels autocracy
> Who cares as long as we
> Wine dine and cheat?

Welcome to Euroland
Can you speak English and
One other tongue?
Let nationality
Local identity
Customs and cultures be
Treated like dung.

Seeing the Light

I stare at the cracks in the ceiling,
Stare at the cracks in the wall.
They look like maps of my feeling,
Not that they read me at all.
I lie on my back without sleeping,
Arms folded under my head,
And think of the hours I've been failing,
Alone fully-clothed on the bed.

I think of myself of all people,
Think of the life I have led,
The troubles I'm in and the trouble
I'll be without when I'm dead.
I stare at the cracks in the ceiling,
My nose and toes in the air,
And if the walls are as blank as I'm feeling
They must be close to despair.

Yes, I'm alive but not kicking,
There's nothing to watch or to do
But hear my wristwatch keep ticking
And think what I think about you.
The bulb in the socket is glowing,
And maybe I'm seeing the light,
But I don't know where I am going
In this black hole of a night.

Sitting on the Harbour Wall

Sitting on the harbour wall
watching the boats go by
looking at waves hitting stone
under a cloudless sky

Sitting on the harbour wall
watching the sun go down
waiting for night to fall
over the sunlit bay

Looking right out to sea
waiting for boats coming home
imagining you and me
sharing these moments alone

Sitting on the harbour wall
knowing it can never be
I'm longing for you to walk
over the waves to me

Sitting on the harbour wall
watching the world go round
waiting for night to fall
over the sunset sea.

On Both Fronts

(Assemblage)

It is at first glimpse a sign
for dangerous bump ahead,
a B lying flat on its back
inside triangular red,
though further down the pole
a similar triangle sign
the other way round or up
is wearing bikini briefs,
silken with lacy frills,
better not taken at speed.

The verso is neither blank
(fixtures and fittings revealed),
nor a version of the front,
no naked back or behind
painted as in 3-D,
but a *trompe l'oeil* pair of breasts,
the isosceles tip below
being painted to represent
a delta of hairy cunt
galvanised onto the pole
that goes through the whole bloody lot,
imagined body and soul
and anything else to impale,
into a concrete and round
pedestal, plinth or base
where both her ankles would be,
were she two-legged and real,
to keep her feet on the ground
and firmly in their place.

And what is the title? Guess.
Topless. Anima. Tat.
Headless. Goddess. Tart.
Totem. Untitled. Tit.
Construction. Erection. Mess.
Woman Wife Mistress Art.
Dada in Mummified Kit.
Muses Useless Unless …

And the artist. Well, let's see …

Put your arm around his shoulder.
It's cold and hard to cry on.

Next of Kin

Is that the telephone or alarm
middle of the night it's three a.m.
the speaker says are you sitting down
I am informed you are next of kin
there is no inoffensive way
to say I'm sorry sorry to say
we have identified your son
he was the victim of a crime
he had an epileptic fit
he hid a weakness of the heart
hit an inoperable growth
a freak wave or an avalanche
he was a criminal doing time
a faulty tyre a rotten branch
he was addicted to his shame
it was a merciful release
he left a suicide note to say
not to worry you weren't to blame
he had a good word for you both
and thanked you for his misspent youth.
I fumble from the bed and feel
the phone that's ringing and for real.

Presences

A father and his adult son
head for the downland's chalky top
and listen to the airborne noise

of ocean-smelling tidal surf
thumping the shingle into cliffs
below the white eroded drop;

admiring both the sun and moon
in equinoctial equipoise
as if ephemeral today,

they stroke the sun-warmed springy turf
on risen seabed where they talk
of miracles by which they lie

on sedimentary layers of chalk
below the cloudless sky-blue sky
remarking on their more than luck,

on golden flowering of the gorse,
the flaming waters, light and dark,
the sundial of the Celtic cross

whose shadow lengthens on the grass,
while in the sea keels under sail
are plying furrows of the waves

and in the sky the jets like stars
heliograph their presences'
evaporating signatures.

Rio Ter

The sunflowers hang their heavy heads,
They hang their heavy heads in shame
For trying to outclimb the sun
Which burns an incandescent flame,
While white birds native to the plain
With slender necks and stork-like frame
Have come to glean a field of grain
As providential for their needs
Before the evening sun goes down.

Water, alluvial and rich,
Alleviates the thirst of trees
Along an irrigation ditch
And fructifies round stone and seed
The flesh of apple and of peach
While green maize drinks the mountain rain
Which runs in silver on the ground
Until the evening sun goes down
And seas are polished by the moon.

WATERCOLOUR

Dreaming of sky or land
as a first or second home,
the sea is marking the sand
with a sinuous rope of foam.

A mouth, an ear, an eye,
the morning glory's view
opens on sea and sky
which mirror forever in blue.

A hawkmoth's hummingbird hum
is eating out of the hand
of a red geranium
in a terracotta stand.

A tangerine hibiscus
is sticking out a tongue
of powder red proboscis
for bees to delve among.

Ceramic villa rooms
look out on a citrus scene
where pink mimosa plumes
foliage feathery green.

Bougainvillaea flowers
photosynthesize
water and sunlit hours
to purple butterflies.

The water's submarine
patterns of turquoise light
are islands of blue and green
in the underwater night.

Parc Liais

Between the port and esplanade,
A granite head commemorates
The naturalist-astronomer,
Emmanuel Liais, former mayor,
With an oasis off the street,
A garden full of tropic trees,
A hothouse of exotic flowers
And, in the grove beyond the lawn,
An ornamental lily pond
In which a central fountain plays.

It is a place where lovers come
To talk and hold each other's hands,
A centrepiece for pensioners,
For friends and midday picnickers
Who choose a seat in sun or shade
And contemplate the play of light
Around the pear-shaped lily pond
Or watch the fountain's plumage change
And hear it imitating rain
While it is glittering in the sun.

So purposefully and in vain
The water droplets rise and pause
In fluctuations of the breeze,
Then fall obedient to the law
Of gravity's near-perfect aim,
Its own musician and applause,
Since water as no artist can
Reciprocates a flawless sky,
Quenches the thirst and can become
The tears and humours of the eye.

Welcome

acidity for rigour
placidity for vigour
flaccidity for figure
welcome middle age!

Exit

No shooting star,
nor late starter,
no young meteor
Knight of the Garter,

no infant prodigy
faithful disciple,
nor young protégé
conquering rival,

no go-getter
snake on the make
enraging tutor,
roué, rake,

no Sunday pundit
flavour of month,
five-minute-wonder
telly dunce,

no family silver
silver spoon,
card on salver
thirst for moon

but Mr Average
long in tooth
trying to salvage
partial truth:

middle-aged plodder
middle of road,
married, mortgaged,
fixed abode,

frightened to dodder
older and odder
into wonder
out of cage.

Why Can't I Be Poet Laureate?

I'm practically unpatriotic.
I prefer the bizarre and neurotic,
I can't ma'am and smarm
Kowtow and salaam,
I prefer my obeisance erotic.

But I'd love all the praise and attention
And the days of poetic ascension
From minimum wage
To media sage
In a world of my own wild invention.

Wine and Cheese

Spare me, oh spare me
The kitschery, the bitchery,
The putschery, the butchery,
The hatchet-job obituary,
The stench of the unsavoury
And overcrowded aviary,
The ludic and the ludicrous,
The Judases and Boudiccas,
The hammy and the homily
And all the Royal Family,
The prudery, the rudery,
The lechery, the pseudery,
The mediocre miseries'
Committees on self-pity
And the alcoholic frolics
Of a melancholic colleague
In the arty-farty party
Of karate literati,
To which if you invite me
I will thank you most politely
And pretend to be delighted
When I haven't been invited.

Self-Deceit

It's not important, neither here nor there.
I do not give a monkey's or a damn.
I am not interested. I do not care.

I am as independent as the air.
The world is full of hypocrites and sham.
It's not important, neither here nor there.

My *raison d'être* would be *laisser faire*
If only I could rise above the jam.
I am not interested. I do not care.

The newspapers are full of the affair.
How many scruples in a milligram?
It's not important, neither here nor there.

Why bother with your looks or what you wear?
The human body is an aging ham.
I am not interested. I do not care.

Beyond the constructs we agree to share
You ask me who on earth I think I am.
It's not important, neither here nor there.
I am not interested. I do not care.

Cyclical

Pending the glow
of a cooling star,
snow and snowdrops
reappear.

A snowflake is caught
in a shivering cobweb,
its filaments taut,
the webster dead.

The grey of rain
flecks green of spruce.
The track to the ruin
is a watercourse.

In yellow cliques
daffodils resurrect
through swanlike necks
their trumpet beaks.

Lilacs perfume
suburban gardens.
Tulips bloom
in scarlet platoons.

Pompoms on chives,
purple coronae,
gild a bee's thighs
for communal honey.

Harvesting midges
haloed by sunset,
swifts are screeches
at slip-catch height.

Wasps in warm beer,
the weir and its DANGER
mean little of either
to trout in the river.

The leaf of a lupin
is drinking a diamond,
a cut-glass button
of rain in its hand.

Smoke from a bonfire
filters the sunlight.
A crane fly whirrs
in grounded flight.

A parliament of starlings
startles the sycamore:
leaves have returned
and started quarrelling.

Water vapour.
Skeletal trees
in greaseproof paper.
Leaf moulds freeze.

Snow and snowdrops
reappear,
pending the glow
of a cooling star.

Song

dear friend
much missed
long time
no see
let's end
this fast
while I'm
still me

no time
like now
while we
exist
to sow
the seeds
get pissed
and how

in end
no sea
no time
so long
no me
no friend
no wine
no song

Fair Copy

(On being asked for two poems in manuscript to be exhibited in the new library of his old school.)

Which of my voices should I choose
To represent me and my views?
The quizzical aimed to perplex?
The puerile obsessed with sex
So both cold frames may gather dust
Round manifestos of dry lust?

Which of my faces shall I wear?
Morose, profane, or debonair?
Should I parade a wound or bruise
For generations to peruse
On library shelves behind a book
As at their mirrored selves they look?

The mystic or the moralist?
The joker or the journalist?
Or sheepish wolf in shepherd's clothing
In love with self and/or self-loathing?
What have I got to gain or hide
From specimens beneath a slide?

After a period of neglect,
My vanity and intellect
Prevaricate and then rejoice
In the dilemmas of the choice.
It is an honour. I accept,
Evasive, humble, proud, inept.

But what if I have not fulfilled
The artistry a schoolboy willed?
What if I have, through failure, failed
With hopes abandoned, faith curtailed,
To ratify the work begun
With one thing to perfection done?

There. It is better said and out;
There is more certainty in doubt
And future perfect time will tell
Whether or what is written well
And if the language lives or dies
With all that it exemplifies.

Words to the living to be read,
These are the poems I have shed,
So let them be a floral wreath
And countersignature to death:
Long live life as long as art
Can liberate the human heart.

A poem
written
in blood
or bone
is not
forgotten
nor alone

in sweat
of art
and hurt
of years
words are wet
with blood
and tears

A poem
learnt
by heart
or hurt
is burnt
for comfort
in the night

and though
the makers
die and go
what the letters
say and do
can console us
dying so

console
atone
and entertain
the soul
in pain
and make us
whole.